A true story from the Bible

DEBORAH
and the
VERY BIG
BATTLE

· WRITTEN BY ·
Tim Thornborough

· ILLUSTRATED BY ·
Jennifer Davison

This is a true story from the Bible about how God's people stopped listening to God and got into a LOT of TROUBLE.

When God speaks, we must always listen carefully. We can always trust what God says because we know that he loves his people and that his words are always true.

So as you read this story, every time someone speaks, put a finger to your lips.

And every time someone listens, put a hand to your ear.

And every time someone does something, point to your hand.

It will remind you that when God speaks, it's important to listen and to do what he says.

Deborah and the Very Big Battle © The Good Book Company, 2020. Reprinted 2021, 2022, 2023.
Words by Tim Thornborough. Illustrations by Jennifer Davison. Design and art direction by André Parker.

thegoodbook.com • thegoodbook.co.uk • thegoodbook.com.au • thegoodbook.co.nz • thegoodbook.co.in

ISBN: 9781784985561 | JOB-007513 | Printed in Turkey.

These are God's people.

And they are in BIG trouble...

God spoke to them,

but they **DID NOT LISTEN.**

They did not do what God said.

They had forgotten that
the word of the Lord is always true,
and that following God's way is the
best thing to do.

And so they started
worshipping pretend gods.

What would God do?

God loved his people.
They needed to learn
they were wrong.

This is Sisera.

Sisera had a huge,
scary army with 900
terrifying iron chariots.

Sisera was cruel and horrible to God's people. He liked nothing better than squishing them and squashing them.

God's people realised how silly and wrong they had been.

They called out to the Lord — the one true God. And God heard them.

And God did something...

This is

DEBORAH.

God sent her to show
his people the way.

When God spoke,

DEBORAH LISTENED.

And Deborah did what God said.

She knew that the word of the Lord is always true, and that following God's way is the best thing to do.

God made Deborah

WISE and FAIR

So all God's people came to her...

...to sort out their arguments and to solve their problems.

But most of all, they came to listen
to the words she spoke from God.

One day, God spoke to Deborah.
And Deborah listened.

And this is what she did...

This is
BARAK.

Deborah told him,

"The Lord commands you to take your men to the top of the mountain. And together we will destroy Sisera and his terrible army."

God's people had no swords.
God's people were few in number.
They had no chariots at all.

But they had something much better.

They had God's promise:
the word of the Lord.

Barak knew that the word of the Lord is always true, and that following God's way is the best thing to do.

So he went, and he asked Deborah to go with him.

At the top of the hill,
they waited and waited.

Sisera's huge, scary army was down below
with his 900 terrifying iron chariots. Barak's
tiny army could never beat Sisera.

But Sisera's mighty army

COULD NEVER BEAT GOD!

At the top of the hill they
waited and waited, until...

GOD
SPOKE.
And Deborah
LISTENED
and did what
God said.

She said to Barak,

"Go! This is the day the Lord has given Sisera into your hands."

BARAK HEARD GOD'S WORD.

Barak trusted God's word.
Barak did what God said.
He opened his mouth
and shouted...

Sisera's huge, scary army was destroyed – and all 900 of his terrifying iron chariots were smashed to pieces.

WHEN GOD SPOKE,

Deborah and Barak

LISTENED.

They trusted God's word.
They did what God said.

Deborah and Barak knew that the word of the Lord is always true, and that following God's way is *always* the best thing to do.

And God gave them

a GREAT VICTORY.

But Sisera ran for his life.

Deborah and Barak sang
a song together.

"When we listen to God's word,
when we trust God's word,
when we obey God's word,
God will give us victory.
Praise the Lord!"

More great books for you to enjoy
in the Very Best Bible Stories series

GOD'S VERY COLOURFUL CREATION
Written By· Tim Thornborough
Illustrated By· Jennifer Davison

DANIEL and the very HUNGRY LIONS
Written By· Tim Thornborough
Illustrated By· Jennifer Davison

DAVID and the very BIG GIANT
Written By· Tim Thornborough
Illustrated By· Jennifer Davison

DEBORAH and the VERY BIG BATTLE
Written By· Tim Thornborough
Illustrated By· Jennifer Davison

ESTHER and the very BRAVE PLAN
Written By· Tim Thornborough
Illustrated By· Jennifer Davison

JONAH and the very BIG FISH
Written By· Tim Thornborough
Illustrated By· Jennifer Davison

MOSES and the VERY BIG RESCUE
Written By· Tim Thornborough
Illustrated By· Jennifer Davison

NOAH and the VERY BIG BOAT
Written By· Tim Thornborough
Illustrated By· Jennifer Davison